APOSTLE MARGUERITE'S BOOK OF SERMONS
VOLUME 1

Apostle Marguerite Breedy-Haynes

Rehoboth Publications
Barbados

APOSTLE MARGUERITE'S BOOK OF SERMONS
VOLUME 1

Rehoboth books may be ordered through Amazon.com and other booksellers.

Breedy-Haynes, Marguerite
Apostle Marguerite's Book Of Sermons
Volume 1

ISBN-13: 9798671123364

Printed in the United States of America

I dedicate this Book to Jesus Christ my Lord and Savior who is the lover of my soul and to the precious Holy Spirit who continues to walk with me and teaches me all things

Contents

Foreword

Romans 10:14 says, " How, then, can they call on the one they have not believed in? And how can they believe in the one of whom they have not heard? And how can they hear without someone preaching to them? The word of God being preached is important for the very reason God gave in Romans 10:14. Each sermon carries the ability to help an individual believe in Jesus and transform their lives.

2 Timothy 3:16-17 also says, "All Scripture is God-breathed and is useful for teaching, rebuking, correcting and training in righteousness, [17] so that the servant of God may be thoroughly equipped for every good work. Here we also learn that the sermon is used for teaching, rebuking, correcting and training in righteousness.

I pray that as you read and apply these sermons to your daily life that you will allow them to not only increase your faith but also carry out a work in you to bring transformation for the sake of the salvation of your soul.

Sermon One

A GOD WHO LISTENS

<u>Psalm 66:18-20</u>

[18] If I had cherished sin in my heart, the Lord would not have listened; [19] but God has surely listened and has heard my prayer. [20] Praise be to God, who has not rejected my prayer or withheld his love from me!

<u>Reference Scriptures</u>

Job 36:21

[21] Beware of turning to evil, which you seem to prefer to affliction.

Isaiah 59:1-2

Surely the arm of the LORD is not too short to save, nor his ear too dull to hear. [2] But your iniquities have separated you from your God; your sins have hidden his face from you, so that he will not hear.

John 9:31

[31] We know that God does not listen to sinners. He listens to the godly person who does his will.

1 John 1:9

[9] If we confess our sins, he is faithful and just and will forgive us our sins and purify us from all unrighteousness.

Isaiah 1:15

¹⁵ When you spread out your hands in prayer, I hide my eyes from you; even when you offer many prayers, I am not listening. Your hands are full of blood!

James 4:3

³ When you ask, you do not receive, because you ask with wrong motives, that you may spend what you get on your pleasures.

Psalm 116:1-2

¹ I love the LORD, for he heard my voice; he heard my cry for mercy. ² Because he turned his ear to me, I will call on him as long as I live.

Psalm 22:24

²⁴ For he has not despised or scorned the suffering of the afflicted one; he has not hidden his face from him but has listened to his cry for help.

Psalm 68:35

³⁵ You, God, are awesome in your sanctuary; the God of Israel gives power and strength to his people. Praise be to God!

Sermon Two

A HEART OF GRATITUDE

Colossians 3:15-17

[15] Let the peace of Christ rule in your hearts, since as members of one body you were called to peace. And be thankful. [16] Let the message of Christ dwell among you richly as you teach and admonish one another with all wisdom through psalms, hymns, and songs from the Spirit, singing to God with gratitude in your hearts. [17] And whatever you do, whether in word or deed, do it all in the name of the Lord Jesus, giving thanks to God the Father through him.

Thanksgiving is always to be given to God the Father, in the name of Jesus, for His mercies. Since all mercies come from, and through him and there is no other way to come to God, we must be grateful and God will always continue to bless a grateful heart. God does not have to do anything for us but He does, so bless and give thanks to Him at all times.

<u>What Happens To An Ungrateful Person?</u>

God called the Israelites an "evil congregation" for their sinful ingratitude (Numbers 14:11-12). To God, an ungrateful attitude is sin—evil—which provokes Him to anger! Although God did not strike Israel with pestilence at that time or disinherit them, He did cause them to wander in the wilderness for 40 additional years, until those that demonstrated this attitude died! Ingratitude will stop your blessings and provoke God's wrath.

<u>**Reference Scriptures**</u>

1 Thessalonians 5:18
"Give thanks in all circumstances; for this is the will of God
in Christ Jesus for you."

Psalm 95:1-3
1 Come, let us sing for joy to the Lord; let us shout aloud to
the Rock of our salvation. 2 Let us come before him with
thanksgiving and extol him with music and song. 3 For
the Lord is the great God, the great King above all gods.

Hebrews 12:28-29
28 Therefore, since we are receiving a kingdom that cannot
be shaken, let us be thankful, and so worship God acceptably
with reverence and awe, 29 for our "God is a consuming fire.

Psalm 100:4-5
4 Enter his gates with thanksgiving and his courts with
praise; give thanks to him and praise his name. 5 For
the Lord is good and his love endures forever; his
faithfulness continues through all generations.

Psalm 118:29
29 Give thanks to the Lord, for he is good; his love endures
forever.

Ephesians 5:20
20 always giving thanks to God the Father for everything, in
the name of our Lord Jesus Christ.

Psalm 136:1-3
1 Give thanks to the Lord, for he is good. His love endures forever. 2 Give thanks to the God of gods. His love endures forever. 3 Give thanks to the Lord of lords: His love endures forever.

ACCEPTING REBUKE FROM GOD CAN ALLOW HIM TO OPEN HIS HEART

Proverbs 1:23-31

[23] Repent at my rebuke! Then I will pour out my thoughts to you, I will make known to you my teachings. [24] But since you refuse to listen when I call and no one pays attention when I stretch out my hand, [25] since you disregard all my advice and do not accept my rebuke. [26] I in turn will laugh when disaster strikes you; I will mock when calamity overtakes you— [27] when calamity overtakes you like a storm, when disaster sweeps over you like a whirlwind,

when distress and trouble overwhelm you. [28] "Then they will call to me but I will not answer; they will look for me but will not find me, [29] since they hated knowledge and did not choose to fear the LORD. [30] Since they would not accept my advice and spurned my rebuke, [31] they will eat the fruit of their ways and be filled with the fruit of their schemes.

WHAT IS A REBUKE"?

To rebuke is to reprimand; strongly warn; restrain.

Reference Scriptures
Hebrews 12:11

No discipline seems pleasant at the time, but painful. Later on, however, it produces a harvest of righteousness and peace for those who have been trained by it

Proverbs 13:18

[18] Whoever disregards discipline comes to poverty and shame, but whoever heeds correction is honored.

2 Timothy 3:16-17

[16] All Scripture is God-breathed and is useful for teaching, rebuking, correcting and training in righteousness, [17] so that the servant of God may be thoroughly equipped for every good work.

Psalm 141:5

[5] Let a righteous man strike me—that is a kindness; let him rebuke me—that is oil on my head. My head will not refuse it, for my prayer will still be against the deeds of evildoers.

Proverbs 19:25

[25] Flog a mocker, and the simple will learn prudence; rebuke the discerning, and they will gain knowledge

Proverbs 25:12

[12] Like an earring of gold or an ornament of fine gold is the rebuke of a wise judge to a listening ear.

Ecclesiastes 7:5

[5] It is better to heed the rebuke of a wise person than to listen to the song of fools.

Proverbs 15:31-32

[31] Whoever heeds life-giving correction will be at home among the wise.

AGE IS JUST A NUMBER FAITH WILL ALLOW YOU TO EXPLORE GREAT THINGS

Joshua 14:6-15

[6] Now the people of Judah approached Joshua at Gilgal, and Caleb son of Jephunneh the Kenizzite said to him, "You know what the LORD said to Moses the man of God at Kadesh Barnea about you and me. [7] I was forty years old when Moses the servant of the LORD sent me from Kadesh Barnea to explore the land. And I brought him back a report according to my convictions, [8] but my fellow Israelites who went up with me made the hearts of the people melt in fear. I, however, followed the LORD my God wholeheartedly. [9] So on that day Moses swore to me, 'The land on which your feet have walked will be your inheritance and that of your children forever, because you have followed the LORD my God wholeheartedly.' [10] "Now then, just as the LORD promised, he has kept me alive for forty-five years since the time he said this to Moses, while Israel moved about in the wilderness. So here I am today, eighty-five years old!

[11] I am still as strong today as the day Moses sent me out; I'm just as vigorous to go out to battle now as I was then. [12] Now give me this hill country that the LORD promised me that day. You yourself heard then that the Anakites were there and their cities were large and fortified, but, the LORD helping me, I will drive them out just as he said." [13] Then Joshua blessed Caleb son of Jephunneh and gave him Hebron as his inheritance. [14] So Hebron has belonged to Caleb son of Jephunneh the Kenizzite

ever since, because he followed the LORD, the God of Israel, wholeheartedly. [15] (Hebron used to be called Kiriath Arba after Arba, who was the greatest man among the Anakites.) Then the land had rest from war.

So often, we hear of people talk about how God used them in the past. They talk about the "glory days" of their youth where they worked tirelessly to spread the Gospel. Their conversation is always in the past. However, the "glory days" do not necessarily have to be in the past. God can still use you, no matter your age. Look at Moses. In Acts 7:23 Moses then ran away and was gone for forty more years before he was approached by God. Moses was 80 years old! In Acts 7:30 Moses was eighty years old, and Aaron eighty-three years old, when they spoke to Pharaoh and in Exodus 7:7 Moses was the leader of his people until he was 120 years old. Moses was 120 years old when he died. His eye were, and his strength was unchanged.

REFERENCE SCRIPTURES

Ruth 4:15
[15] He will renew your life and sustain you in your old age. For your daughter-in-law, who loves you and who is better to you than seven sons, has given him birth."

Psalm 92:14
[14] They will still bear fruit in old age; they will stay fresh and green,

Psalm 71:18-19

¹⁸ Even when I am old and gray, do not forsake me, my God, till I declare your power to the next generation, your mighty acts to all who are to come.

Philemon 1:9

⁹ yet I prefer to appeal to you on the basis of love. It is as none other than Paul—an old man and now also a prisoner of Christ Jesus—

Isaiah 46:4

And I will still be carrying you when you are old. Your hair will turn gray, and I will still carry you. I made you, and I will carry you to safety.

ALLOW THOSE AROUND YOU TO ANOINT YOUR BABY

<u>Luke 1:39-45</u>

[39] At that time Mary got ready and hurried to a town in the hill country of Judea, [40] where she entered Zechariah's home and greeted Elizabeth. [41] When Elizabeth heard Mary's greeting, the baby leaped in her womb, and Elizabeth was filled with the Holy Spirit. [42] In a loud voice she exclaimed: "Blessed are you among women, and blessed is the child you will bear! [43] But why am I so favored, that the mother of my Lord should come to me? [44] As soon as the sound of your greeting reached my ears, the baby in my womb leaped for joy. [45] Blessed is she who has believed that the Lord would fulfill his promises to her!"

As we fellowship or spend time with a person then we pick up things from one another. We kind of pick up parts of a person's character and personality. Sometimes the things we pick up from one another maybe good and at other times it may not be good. Therefore, we must seek God and choose careful who we seek to have among us daily. Seek God first and ask Him for builders and not destroyers of your life.

<u>REFERENCE SCRIPTURE</u>

Proverbs 27:17
[17] As iron sharpens iron, so one person sharpens another.

Ephesians 4:29
Do not let any unwholesome talk come out of your mouths,
but only what is helpful for building others up according to
their needs, that it may benefit those who listen.

Romans 14:19
So then, we pursue the things, which make for peace and the
building up of one another.

Proverbs 12:26
The righteous choose their friends carefully, but the way of
the wicked leads them astray.

1 Thessalonians 5:11
Therefore, encourage one another and build each other up as
you are already doing.

1 Thessalonians 4:18
Therefore, encourage one another with these words.

Proverbs 27:9
Ointments and perfume encourage the heart; in a similar
way, a friend's advice is sweet to the soul.

ANYONE WHO WANTS TO BE GREAT IN GOD MUST BECOME A CHILD

<u>Matthew 18:1-9</u>

At that time, the disciples came to Jesus and asked, "Who, then, is the greatest in the kingdom of heaven?" [2] He called a little child to him, and placed the child among them. [3] And he said: "Truly I tell you, unless you change and become like little children, you will never enter the kingdom of heaven. [4] Therefore, whoever takes the lowly position of this child is the greatest in the kingdom of heaven. [5] And whoever welcomes one such child in my name welcomes me.

[6] "If anyone causes one of these little ones—those who believe in me—to stumble, it would be better for them to have a large millstone hung around their neck and to be drowned in the depths of the sea. [7] Woe to the world because of the things that cause people to stumble! Such things must come, but woe to the person through whom they come! [8] If your hand or your foot causes you to stumble, cut it off and throw it away. It is better for you to enter life maimed or crippled than to have two hands or two feet and be thrown into eternal fire. [9] And if your eye causes you to stumble, gouge it out and throw it away. It is better for you to enter life with one eye than to have two eyes and be thrown into the fire of hell.

Jesus says that we will not enter the kingdom of heaven unless we become like a child. We need to change our mindset and think as children think. Not that we become immature and act childish, but that we accept things in simplicity and humility. Children have a way of believing everything you say and they are quick to return after being punished. This moves God's heart, so we must seek to be humble.

<u>REFERENCE SCRIPTURES</u>

1 Peter 5:6
[6] Humble yourselves, therefore, under God's mighty hand, that he may lift you up in due time.

James 4:10
[10] Humble yourselves before the Lord, and he will lift you up.

Isaiah 58:5
[5] Is this the kind of fast I have chosen, only a day for people to humble themselves? Is it only for bowing one's head like a reed and for lying in sackcloth and ashes? Is that what you call a fast, a day acceptable to the LORD?

Daniel 10:12
[12] Then he continued, "Do not be afraid, Daniel. Since the first day that you set your mind to gain understanding and to humble yourself before your God, your words were heard, and I have come in response to them.

Isaiah 66:2
[2] Has not my hand made all these things, and so they came into being?" declares the LORD. "These are the ones I look on with favor: those who are humble and contrite in spirit, and who tremble at my word.

Matthew 23:12
¹² For those who exalt themselves will be humbled, and those
who humble themselves will be exalted.

Psalm 147:6
⁶ The LORD sustains the humble
but casts the wicked to the ground.

ANYTHING THAT GOD PLACED INSIDE OF YOU TO IMPACT THE WORLD CANNOT BE CONTAMINATED

Matthew 1:21-25

[21] She will give birth to a son, and you are to give him the name Jesus, because he will save his people from their sins." [22] All this took place to fulfill what the Lord had said through the prophet: [23] "The virgin will conceive and give birth to a son, and they will call him Immanuel" (which means "God with us"). [24] When Joseph woke up, he did what the angel of the Lord had commanded him and took Mary home as his wife. [25] But he did not consummate their marriage until she gave birth to a son. And he gave him the name Jesus.

God places you into His perfect will for your life, then He will lead you into the divine plan and destiny that He has set up for your life. And in that divine destiny will be your call, your missions, your divine assignments, and the specific people that He will want you to work with and your anointing. Though we are to be actively involved **"in"** the world to the degree that God will lead us to, we also have to protect what God has given to us from contamination.

REFERENCE SCRIPTURES

Isaiah 52:11

Depart, depart, go out from there, Touch nothing unclean;
Go out of the midst of her, purify yourselves, You who carry
the vessels of the LORD.

James 1:27
Religion that God our Father accepts as pure and faultless is this: to look after orphans and widows in their distress and to keep oneself from being polluted by the world.

Acts 15:20
But that we write to them that, they abstain from things contaminated by idols and from fornication and from what is strangled and from blood.

2 Corinthians 6:17
"Therefore come out from among them and be separate, says the Lord. Touch no unclean thing, and I will receive you."

Numbers 8:6
"Take the Levites from among the Israelites and make them ceremonially clean.

ANYTIME THE DEVIL WANTS TO DESTROY YOU, HE'LL SEND SOMEONE TO TRAP AND ENSLAVE YOU

Judges 16:1-20

One day Samson went to Gaza, where he saw a prostitute. He went in to spend the night with her. [2] The people of Gaza were told, "Samson is here!" So they surrounded the place and lay in wait for him all night at the city gate. They made no move during the night, saying, "At dawn we'll kill him."[3] But Samson lay there only until the middle of the night. Then he got up and took hold of the doors of the city gate, together with the two posts, and tore them loose, bar and all. He lifted them to his shoulders and carried them to the top of the hill that faces Hebron. [4] Some time later, he fell in love with a woman in the Valley of Sorek whose name was Delilah. [5] The rulers of the Philistines went to her and said, "See if you can lure him into showing you the secret of his great strength and how we can overpower him so we may tie him up and subdue him. Each one of us will give you eleven hundred shekels of silver."

[6] So Delilah said to Samson, "Tell me the secret of your great strength and how you can be tied up and subdued."[7] Samson answered her, "If anyone ties me with seven fresh bowstrings that have not been dried, I'll become as weak as any other man." [8] Then the rulers of the Philistines brought her seven fresh bowstrings that had not been dried, and she tied him with them. [9] With men hidden in the room, she called to him, "Samson, the Philistines are upon you!" But he snapped the bowstrings as easily as a piece of string snaps when it comes close to a flame. So the secret of his strength was not discovered.

[10] Then Delilah said to Samson, "You have made a fool of me; you lied to me. Come now; tell me how you can be tied."

[11] He said, "If anyone ties me securely with new ropes that have never been used, I'll become as weak as any other man." [12] So Delilah took new ropes and tied him with them. Then, with men hidden in the room, she called to him, "Samson, the Philistines are upon you!" But he snapped the ropes off his arms as if they were threads. [13] Delilah then said to Samson, "All this time you have been making a fool of me and lying to me. Tell me how you can be tied." He replied, "If you weave the seven braids of my head into the fabric on the loom and tighten it with the pin, I'll become as weak as any other man." So while he was sleeping, Delilah took the seven braids of his head, wove them into the fabric [14] and tightened it with the pin.

Again, she called to him, "Samson, the Philistines are upon you!" He awoke from his sleep and pulled up the pin and the loom, with the fabric. [15] Then she said to him, "How can you say, 'I love you,' when you won't confide in me? This is the third time you have made a fool of me and haven't told me the secret of your great strength."

[16] With such nagging she prodded him day after day until he was sick to death of it. [17] So he told her everything. "No razor has ever been used on my head," he said, "because I have been a Nazirite dedicated to God from my mother's womb. If my head were shaved, my strength would leave me, and I would become as weak as any other man." [18] When Delilah saw that he had told her everything, she sent word to the rulers of the Philistines, "Come back once more; he has told me everything." So the rulers of the Philistines returned with the silver in their hands. [19] After putting him to sleep on her lap, she called for someone to shave off the seven braids of his hair, and so began to subdue him. And his strength left him. [20] Then she called, "Samson, the Philistines are upon you!" He awoke from his sleep and thought, "I'll go out

as before and shake myself free." But he did not know that the LORD had left him.

<u>Reference Scriptures</u>

1 Samuel 23:26
²⁶ Saul was going along one side of the mountain, and David and his men were on the other side, hurrying to get away from Saul. As Saul and his forces were closing in on David and his men to capture them,

Psalm 118:10-12
¹⁰ All the nations surrounded me, but in the name of the LORD, I cut them down. ¹¹ They surrounded me on every side, but in the name of the LORD, I cut them down. ¹² They swarmed around me like bees, but they were consumed as quickly as burning thorns; in the name of the LORD I cut them down.

Acts 9:24
²⁴ but Saul learned of their plan. Day and night, they kept close watch on the city gates in order to kill him.

BE AN AID AND GOD WILL BLESS YOU

Joshua 1:1-6 & 16-18

After the death of Moses the servant of the LORD, the LORD said to Joshua son of Nun, Moses' aide: ² "Moses my servant is dead. Now then, you and all these people, get ready to cross the Jordan River into the land I am about to give to them—to the Israelites. ³ I will give you every place where you set your foot, as I promised Moses. ⁴ Your territory will extend from the desert to Lebanon, and from the great river, the Euphrates—all the Hittite country—to the Mediterranean Sea in the west. ⁵ No one will be able to stand against you all the days of your life. As I was with Moses, so I will be with you; I will never leave you nor forsake you. ⁶ Be strong and courageous, because you will lead these people to inherit the land I swore to their ancestors to give them.

¹⁶ Then they answered Joshua, "Whatever you have commanded us we will do, and wherever you send us we will go. ¹⁷ Just as we fully obeyed Moses, so we will obey you. Only may the LORD your God be with you as he was with Moses. ¹⁸ Whoever rebels against your word and does not obey it, whatever you may command them, will be put to death. Only be strong and courageous!"

WHAT IS AN AID?

An aid is someone who lends assistance or help to someone in order for them to fulfil their goals.

Joshua served Moses until he died. Joshua was always willing to go the second mile. He knew whom he served and that He was an assistant to Moses, serving God! Although Moses tarried with God on the mountain for forty days and forty nights, Joshua waited patiently for his return. Joshua just served; he neither pushed for position, nor pushed himself ahead of the man of God. He was a true servant with a servant's heart and that is why God promoted him.

REFERENCE SCRIPTURES

Mark 9:35
Sitting down, He called the twelve and said to them, "If anyone wants to be first, he shall be last of all and servant of all."

Matthew 23:11
"But the greatest among you shall be your servant.

Mark 10:44
and whoever wishes to be first among you shall be slave of all.

Philippians 2:7
but emptied Himself, taking the form of a bond-servant, and being made in the likeness of men.

Romans 1:1
Paul, a bond-servant of Christ Jesus, called as an apostle, set apart for the gospel of God,

Numbers 11:28
Then Joshua the son of Nun, the attendant of Moses from his youth, said, "Moses, my lord, restrain them."

Proverbs 14:35
The king's favor is toward a servant who acts wisely, but his
anger is toward him who acts shamefully.

Isaiah 52:13
Behold, My servant will prosper, He will be high and lifted
up and greatly exalted.

Hebrews 3:5
Now Moses was faithful in all His house as a servant, for a
testimony of those things which were to be spoken later

Jude 1:1
Jude, a bond-servant of Jesus Christ, and brother of James,
To those who are the called, beloved in God the Father, and
kept for Jesus Christ:

2 Peter 1:1
Simon Peter, a bond-servant and apostle of Jesus Christ, To
those who have received a faith of the same kind as ours, by the
righteousness of our God and Savior, Jesus Christ:

BE CAREFUL OF THE WORDS THE ENEMY WILL USE TO STOP YOUR DESTINY

<u>Genesis 3:1-20</u>

Now the serpent was more crafty than any of the wild animals the LORD God had made. He said to the woman, "Did God really say, 'You must not eat from any tree in the garden'?" ² The woman said to the serpent, "We may eat fruit from the trees in the garden, ³ but God did say, 'You must not eat fruit from the tree that is in the middle of the garden, and you must not touch it, or you will die.'" ⁴ "You will not certainly die," the serpent said to the woman. ⁵ "For God knows that when you eat from it your eyes will be opened, and you will be like God, knowing good and evil."

⁶ When the woman saw that the fruit of the tree was good for food and pleasing to the eye, and also desirable for gaining wisdom, she took some and ate it. She also gave some to her husband, who was with her, and he ate it. ⁷ Then the eyes of both of them were opened, and they realized they were naked; so they sewed fig leaves together and made coverings for themselves. ⁸ Then the man and his wife heard the sound of the LORD God as he was walking in the garden in the cool of the day, and they hid from the LORD God among the trees of the garden. ⁹ But the LORD God called to the man, "Where are you?"¹⁰ He answered, "I heard you in the garden, and I was afraid because I was naked; so I hid."

¹¹ And he said, "Who told you that you were naked? Have you eaten from the tree that I commanded you not to eat from?" ¹² The man said, "The woman you put here with me—she gave

me some fruit from the tree, and I ate it." [13] Then the LORD God said to the woman, "What is this you have done?" The woman said, "The serpent deceived me, and I ate." [14] So the LORD God said to the serpent, "Because you have done this, "Cursed are you above all livestock and all wild animals! You will crawl on your belly and you will eat dust all the days of your life. [15] And I will put enmity between you and the woman, and between your offspring and hers; he will crush your head, and you will strike his heel."

[16] To the woman he said, "I will make your pains in childbearing very severe; with painful labor you will give birth to children. Your desire will be for your husband, and he will rule over you." [17] To Adam he said, "Because you listened to your wife and ate fruit from the tree about which I commanded you, 'You must not eat from it,' "Cursed is the ground because of you; through painful toil you will eat food from it all the days of your life. [18] It will produce thorns and thistles for you, and you will eat the plants of the field. [19] By the sweat of your brow you will eat your food until you return to the ground, since from it you were taken; for dust you are and to dust you will return." [20] Adam named his wife Eve, because she would become the mother of all the living.

<u>Reference Scriptures</u>

John 10:4-5
[4] When he has brought out all his own, he goes on ahead of them, and his sheep follow him because they know his voice. [5] But they will never follow a stranger; in fact, they will run away from him because they do not recognize a stranger's voice."

John 10:27-28
²⁷ My sheep listen to my voice; I know them, and they
follow me. ²⁸ I give them eternal life, and they shall never
perish; no one will snatch them out of my hand.

John 10:3
³ The gatekeeper opens the gate for him, and the sheep listen
to his voice. He calls his own sheep by name and leads them
out.

Genesis 27:8
Now, my son, listen carefully and do what I tell you:

BEING COMPASSIONATE AND KIND

Colossians 3:12-15

[12] Therefore, as God's chosen people, holy and dearly loved, clothe yourselves with compassion, kindness, humility, gentleness and patience. [13] Bear with each other and forgive one another if any of you has a grievance against someone. Forgive as the Lord forgave you. [14] And over all these virtues put on love, which binds them all together in perfect unity. [15] Let the peace of Christ rule in your hearts, since as members of one body you were called to peace. And be thankful.

<u>WHY SHOULD WE PUT ON COMPASSION?</u>

The Hebrew and Greek words translated "compassion" in the Bible mean "to have mercy, to feel sympathy and to have pity." We should be compassionate towards others because according to the Bible, God is "a compassionate and gracious God, slow to anger, abounding in love and faithfulness" (Psalm 86:15). Like all of God's attributes, His compassion is infinite and eternal. His compassions never fail; they are new every morning (Lamentations 3:22-23) and as His children we should have His attributes.

Matthew 5:41
If anyone forces you to go one mile, go with them two miles.

<u>EXAMPLES OF PEOPLE BEING COMPASSIONATE</u>

Jesus had compassion on the sick (Matthew 14:13-14). Jesus had compassion on the demon-possessed (Mark 5:18-19; Mark 9:20-22). Jesus had compassion on those who were hurt (Luke 10:33-35). Jesus had compassion on the wayward (Luke 15:20-24). Jesus had compassion on the hungry (Matthew 15:32; see also Mark 6:34 and Mark 8:1-8).

The Good Samaritan-Luke 10:25-37

Ruth had compassion for Naomi- Ruth chapter 1

Job had compassion on the poor- Job 31:16

<u>BENEFITS OF COMPASSION</u>

<u>Good will come to you</u>

Psalm 112:4-5

[4] Even in darkness light dawns for the upright, for those who are gracious and compassionate and righteous. [5] Good will come to those who are generous and lend freely, who conduct their affairs with justice.

<u>You will fulfill the law of Christ</u>

Galatians 6:2

[2] Carry each other's burdens, and in this way you will fulfill the law of Christ.

<u>God will comfort you In Trouble Times</u>

2 Corinthians 1:3-4

[3] Praise be to the God and Father of our Lord Jesus Christ, the Father of compassion and the God of all comfort, [4] who comforts us in all our troubles, so that we can comfort those in any trouble with the comfort we ourselves receive from God.

<u>You will be united with Jesus and be comforted by His love</u>

Philippians 2:1-2

Therefore if you have any encouragement from being united with Christ, if any comfort from his love, if any common sharing in the Spirit, if any tenderness and compassion, **2** then make my joy complete by being like-minded, having the same love, being one in spirit and of one mind.

<u>Reference Scriptures</u>

<u>Ephesians 4:32</u>

Be kind and compassionate to one another, forgiving each other, just as in Christ God forgave you.

<u>1 Peter 3:8</u>

Finally, all of you, be like-minded, be sympathetic, love one another, be compassionate and humble.

<u>Zechariah 7:9-10</u>

This is what the Lord Almighty said: 'Administer true justice; show mercy and compassion to one another. Do not oppress the widow or the fatherless, the foreigner or the poor. Do not plot evil against each other.'

<u>1 John 3:17</u>

If anyone has material possessions and sees a brother or sister in need but has no pity on them, how can the love of God be in that person?

BEING CONFIDENT OF WHO YOU ARE IN GOD

ROMANS 8:31-39

[31] What, then, shall we say in response to these things? If God is for us, who can be against us? [32] He who did not spare his own Son, but gave him up for us all—how will he not also, along with him, graciously give us all things? [33] Who will bring any charge against those whom God has chosen? It is God who justifies. [34] Who then is the one who condemns? No one. Christ Jesus who died—more than that, who was raised to life—is at the right hand of God and is also interceding for us. [35] Who shall separate us from the love of Christ? Shall trouble or hardship or persecution or famine or nakedness or danger or sword? [36] As it is written:

"For your sake we face death all day long; we are considered as sheep to be slaughtered." [37] No, in all these things we are more than conquerors through him who loved us. [38] For I am convinced that neither death nor life, neither angels nor demons, neither the present nor the future, nor any powers, [39] neither height nor depth, nor anything else in all creation, will be able to separate us from the love of God that is in Christ Jesus our Lord.

God is able to do all things and if your identity is in Him, you should be confident. A lot of time, people have confidence in the wrong things; for instance, people have confidence in unreliable things like fellow human, their wealth, the economy, government, educational certificates and others. The only person to have confidence in is God.

Confidence in God is so powerful, unshakeable and rock solid because He never fails.

<u>REFERENCE SCRIPTURES</u>

1 John 4:17
17 This is how love is made complete among us so that we will have confidence on the Day of Judgment: In this world we are like Jesus.

1 John 5:14
14 This is the confidence we have in approaching God: that if we ask anything according to his will, he hears us.

2 Chronicles 32:8
8 With him is only the arm of flesh, but with us is the LORD our God to help us and to fight our battles." And the people gained confidence from what Hezekiah the king of Judah said.

Ephesians 3:12
12 In him and through faith in him we may approach God with freedom and confidence.

Hebrews 4:16
16 Let us then approach God's throne of grace with confidence, so that we may receive mercy and find grace to help us in our time of need.

Isaiah 32:17
17 The fruit of that righteousness will be peace; its effect will be quietness and confidence forever.

Jeremiah 17:7
7 "But blessed is the one who trusts in the LORD, whose confidence is in him.

Nehemiah 6:16
16 When all our enemies heard about this, all the surrounding nations were afraid and lost their self-confidence, because they realized that this work had been done with the help of our God.

Philippians 1:6
6 being confident of this, that he who began a good work in you will carry it on to completion until the day of Christ Jesus.

CALLING OUT TO GOD

<u>Jeremiah 33:1-6</u>

While Jeremiah was still confined in the courtyard of the guard, the word of the LORD came to him a second time. [2] "This is what the LORD says, he who made the earth, the LORD who formed it and established it—the LORD is his name. [3] 'Call to me and I will answer you and tell you great and unsearchable things you do not know.' [4] For this is what the LORD, the God of Israel, says about the houses in this city and the royal palaces of Judah that have been torn down to be used against the siege ramps and the sword [5] in the fight with the Babylonians. 'They will be filled with the dead bodies of the people I will slay in my anger and wrath. I will hide my face from this city because of all its wickedness. [6] "'Nevertheless, I will bring health and healing to it; I will heal my people and will let them enjoy abundant peace and security.

Calling out to God is an act of desperation and total concentration. It is a fervent expression of faith in God and trust in His goodness and power to act on your behalf.

What must you do when calling out to God? There must be:
- **Genuine humility**
- **Unconditional surrender**
- **A plea for mercy**
- **Personal helplessness**
- **Faith in God's power and resources**

<u>Reference Scriptures</u>

2 Chronicles 7:14
[14] if my people, who are called by my name, will humble themselves and pray and seek my face and turn from their wicked ways, then I will hear from heaven, and I will forgive their sin and will heal their land.

Psalms 79:6
Pour out Your wrath upon the nations which do not know You, And upon the kingdoms which do not call upon Your name.

Psalms 50:15
Call upon Me in the day of trouble; I shall rescue you, and you will honor Me."

Isaiah 55:6
[6] Seek the LORD while he may be found; call on him while he is near.

Jeremiah 29:12
[12] Then you will call on me and come and pray to me, and I will listen to you.

Genesis 26:25
[25] Isaac built an altar there and called on the name of the LORD. There he pitched his tent, and there his servants dug a well.

Psalms 86:5
For You, Lord, are good, and ready to forgive, And abundant in lovingkindness to all who call upon You.

Psalms 116:2
Because He has inclined His ear to me, Therefore I shall call
upon Him as long as I live.

Job 27:10
"Will he take delight in the Almighty? Will he call on God
at all times?

2 Timothy 2:22
Now flee from youthful lusts and pursue righteousness,
faith, love and peace, with those who call on the Lord from a
pure heart.

Lamentations 3:55
I called on Your name, O LORD, Out of the lowest pit.

2 Samuel 22:4
"I call upon the LORD, who is worthy to be praised, And I
am saved from my enemies.

Psalms 18:3
I call upon the LORD, who is worthy to be praised, And I
am saved from my enemies.

1 Kings 18:24
"Then you call on the name of your god, and I will call on
the name of the LORD, and the God who answers by fire, He is
God." And all the people said, "That is a good idea."

Psalms 18:6
In my distress I called upon the LORD, And cried to my
God for help; He heard my voice out of His temple, And my
cry for help before Him came into His ears.

Psalms 28:1-2
To You, O LORD, I call; My rock, do not be deaf to me, For
if You are silent to me, I will become like those who go down
to the pit. Hear the voice of my supplications when I cry to You
for help, When I lift up my hands toward Your holy sanctuary.

Psalms 55:16
As for me, I shall call upon God, And the LORD will save
me.

Psalms 91:15
"He will call upon Me, and I will answer him; I will be with
him in trouble; I will rescue him and honor him.

Psalms 120:1
In my trouble I cried to the LORD, And He answered me.

Isaiah 65:24
"It will also come to pass that before they call, I will answer;
and while they are still speaking, I will hear.

Jeremiah 33:3
'Call to Me and I will answer you, and I will tell you great
and mighty things, which you do not know.'

Acts 2:21
And everyone who calls on the name of the Lord will be
saved.

Romans 10:12-14
For there is no distinction between Jew and Greek; for the
same Lord is Lord of all, abounding in riches for all who call on
Him; for "WHOEVER WILL CALL ON THE NAME OF THE

LORD WILL BE SAVED." How then will they call on Him in whom they have not believed? How will they believe in Him whom they have not heard? And how will they hear without a preacher?

CAN A CHRISTIAN LOSE HIS OR HER SALVATION?

<u>Matthew 7:19-23</u>

19 Every tree that does not bear good fruit is cut down and thrown into the fire. 20 Thus, by their fruit you will recognize them. 21 "Not everyone who says to me, 'Lord, Lord,' will enter the kingdom of heaven, but only the one who does the will of my Father who is in heaven. 22 Many will say to me on that day, 'Lord, Lord, did we not prophesy in your name and in your name drive out demons and in your name perform many miracles?' 23 Then I will tell them plainly, 'I never knew you. Away from me, you evildoers!'

In 1 Timothy 1:18-20, Paul warned Timothy to keep the faith and to keep a good conscience, and to be reminded of those who did not. The Apostle refers to those who made "shipwreck of their faith," men whom he "handed over to Satan that they may learn not to blaspheme." This passage is a sober warning with concrete examples of those who fell away grievously from their Christian profession. There is no question that professing believers can fall and fall radically. We think of men like Peter, for example, who denied Christ. However, the fact that he was restored shows that not every professing believer who falls has fallen past the point of no return if they repent.

<u>Reference Scriptures</u>
1 Timothy 1:19

19 holding on to faith and a good conscience, which some have rejected and so have suffered shipwreck with regard to the faith.

1 Timothy 6:21
21 which some have professed and in so doing have
departed from the faith.

2 Timothy 2:18
18 who have departed from the truth. They say that the
resurrection has already taken place, and they destroy the
faith of some.

2 Corinthians 13:5
5 Examine yourselves to see whether you are in the faith;
test yourselves. Do you not realize that Christ Jesus is in
you—unless, of course, you fail the test?

Lamentations 3:40
40 Let us examine our ways and test them, and let us return
to the LORD.

1 Corinthians 9:27
No, I discipline my body and make it my slave, so that after
I have preached to others, I myself will not be disqualified.

CHANGE WILL COME WHEN WE LEARN TO SACRIFICE

Romans 12:1

"Therefore, I urge you, brothers and sisters, in view of God's mercy, to offer your bodies as a living sacrifice, holy and pleasing to God—this is your true and proper worship"

Every day God wants us to offer our bodies as living sacrifices to God. The Lord does not force His children to obey Him; rather He longs for us to choose His ways over our own desires. Our sacrifice of <u>living for Jesus</u> on a daily basis in spite of the temptations, trials, and tragedies of life encourages an investment of sacrifice with an eternity of rewards and many changes in our lives.

REFERENCE SCRIPTURES

Psalm 51:17
"My sacrifice, O God, is a broken spirit; a broken and contrite heart you, God, will not despise"

Hebrews 13:15
"Through Jesus, therefore, let us continually offer to God a sacrifice of praise—the fruit of lips that openly profess his name"

Hebrews 13:16
"And do not forget to do good and to share with others, for with such sacrifices God is pleased"

CHARACTERISTICS OF A PERSON WHO IS FILLED WITH THE SPIRIT

<u>Micah 3:8</u>

On the other hand, I am filled with power-- With the Spirit of the LORD-- And with justice and courage to make known to Jacob his rebellious act, Even to Israel his sin.

The word of God said that you will know them by their fruit and God wants us all to be filled with His spirit so that we can bring glory to His name in the earth. Here are ten characteristics of a spirit filled Christian.

1. Operating in the fruit of the spirit
2. Seeks to build the Kingdom of God
3. Filled with and live by the word of God
4. Submits to God as Master.
5. Being in constant prayer
6. Obedient to spiritual Authority
7. Avoids quarrels and useless arguments
8. Demonstrates justice
9. Operates in Miracles, signs and wonders
10. Is Committed – SUFFERS WHATEVER, WHENEVER NECESSARY for God's work.

<u>REFERENCE SCRIPTURES</u>

<u>Galatians 5:16-17</u>

But I say, walk by the Spirit, and you will not carry out the desire of the flesh. For the flesh sets its desire against the Spirit, and the Spirit against the flesh; for these are in opposition to one another, so that you may not do the things that you please.

Galatians 5:22-24
But the fruit of the Spirit is love, joy, peace, patience, kindness, goodness, faithfulness, gentleness, self-control; against such things there is no law. Now those who belong to Christ Jesus have crucified the flesh with its passions and desires.

Galatians 5:25
If we live by the Spirit, let us also walk by the Spirit.

Ephesians 5:18
And do not get drunk with wine, for that is dissipation, but be filled with the Spirit,

Galatians 6:8,
"He that sows to the Spirit will of the Spirit reap everlasting life" –

Sermon Seventeen

CLEAN UP YOURSELF AND AVAIL YOURSELF TO GOD

2 Timothy 2:20-21

[20] In a large house there are articles not only of gold and silver, but also of wood and clay; some are for special purposes and some for common use. [21] Those who cleanse themselves from the latter will be instruments for special purposes, made holy, useful to the Master and prepared to do any good work.

All of God's people are a vessel of some kind. Either we are a vessel that brings honor to Him, or we are a vessel that dishonors His name. Which kind of vessel are you? Paul teaches us what God expects of each of us in his instructions to Timothy, a young minister of the Lord. We need to apply this teaching by being honest with ourselves about the things that God wants us to remove from our lives and begin to renounce and denounce them so that the Holy Spirit can help us to get rid of the hindrances and allow us to be clean vessels for God.

<u>REFERENCE SCRIPTURES</u>

2 Corinthians 7:1
Therefore, since we have these promises, dear friends, let us purify ourselves from everything that contaminates body and spirit, perfecting holiness out of reverence for God.

1 John 3:3
And everyone who has this hope in Him purifies himself, just as He is pure.

1 Thessalonians 4:7
⁷ For God did not call us to be impure, but to live a holy life

2 Corinthians 7:1
Having therefore these promises, dearly beloved, let us cleanse ourselves from all filthiness of the flesh and spirit, perfecting holiness in the fear of God.

Mark 7:20-23
And he said, That which cometh out of the man, that defiles the man. For from within, out of the heart of men, proceed evil thoughts, adulteries, fornications, murders, Thefts, covetousness, wickedness, deceit, lasciviousness, an evil eye, blasphemy, pride, foolishness: All these evil things come from within, and defile the man.

COME OUT FROM AMONG THEM, YOU WHO CARRY THE VESSEL OF THE LORD

We are admonished to keep ourselves clean from the pollutions of the world. It is a call to all in the bondage of sin and satan, to use the liberty Christ has proclaimed. We are not to lose time nor linger. Those in the way of duty are under God's special protection; and he that believes this, will not operate in fear knowing that God has their back.

Isaiah 52.8-12

Listen! Your watchmen lift up their voices; together they shout for joy. When the LORD returns to Zion, they will see it with their own eyes. [9] Burst into songs of joy together, you ruins of Jerusalem, for the LORD has comforted his people, he has redeemed Jerusalem. [10] The LORD will lay bare his holy arm in the sight of all the nations, and all the ends of the earth will see the salvation of our God. Depart, depart, go out from there! Touch no unclean thing! Come out from it and be pure, you who carry the articles of the LORD's house. [12] But you will not leave in haste or go in flight; for the LORD will go before you, the God of Israel will be your rear guard.

Rear guard is a group of soldiers who are placed at the back of an army to protect the army from being attacked from behind

Reference Scriptures
2 Timothy 2:21
[21] Those who cleanse themselves from the latter will be instruments for special purposes, made holy, useful to the Master and prepared to do any good work.

Isaiah 48:20

²⁰ Leave Babylon, flee from the Babylonians! Announce this
with shouts of joy
and proclaim it. Send it out to the ends of the earth; say,
"The LORD has redeemed his servant Jacob."

Isaiah 1:16

¹⁶ Wash and make yourselves clean. Take your evil deeds
out of my sight; stop doing wrong.

2 Corinthians 6:17

¹⁷ Therefore, "Come out from them and be separate, says the
Lord. Touch no unclean thing, and I will receive you."

2 Timothy 2:19

¹⁹ Nevertheless, God's solid foundation stands firm, sealed
with this inscription: "The Lord knows those who are his," and,
"Everyone who confesses the name of the Lord must turn away
from wickedness."

Micah 2:13

¹³ The One who breaks open the way will go up before them;
they will break through the gate and go out. Their King will
pass through before them, the LORD at their head."

Exodus 14:19

¹⁹ Then the angel of God, who had been traveling in front of
Israel's army, withdrew and went behind them. The pillar of
cloud also moved from in front and stood behind them,

Jeremiah 15:17

[17] I never sat in the company of revelers, never made merry with them; I sat alone because your hand was on me and you had filled me with indignation.

Revelation 18:4

Then I heard another voice from heaven say: "Come out of her, my people, so that you will not share in her sins or contract any of her plagues.

Leviticus 20:23-26

[23] You must not live according to the customs of the nations I am going to drive out before you. Because they did all these things, I abhorred them. [24] But I said to you, "You will possess their land; I will give it to you as an inheritance, a land flowing with milk and honey." I am the LORD your God, who has set you apart from the nations. [25] "'You must therefore make a distinction between clean and unclean animals and between unclean and clean birds. Do not defile yourselves by any animal or bird or anything that moves along the ground—those that I have set apart as unclean for you. [26] You are to be holy to me because I, the LORD, am holy, and I have set you apart from the nations to be my own.

2 Corinthians 6:14

[14] Do not be yoked together with unbelievers. For what do righteousness and wickedness have in common? Or what fellowship can light have with darkness?

Deuteronomy 23:6

[6] Do not seek a treaty of friendship with them as long as you live.

Sermon Nineteen

COMPLACENCY AND THE COMING OF THE LORD

Luke 12:47-48

[47] "The servant who knows the master's will and does not get ready or does not do what the master wants will be beaten with many blows. [48] But the one who does not know and does things deserving punishment will be beaten with few blows. From everyone who has been given much, much will be demanded; and from the one who has been entrusted with much, much more will be asked.

Complacency is a feeling of being satisfied with how things are and not wanting to try to make them better, while unaware of some potential danger.

Complacency is dangerous because, as the definition says, we have some 'sense' of security- but there is impending danger. In the spiritual life, there is no standing still – only moving forward or going back. If we get complacent, we may find that we have become lukewarm, numb, and a lot further from Christ than we want to be.

Far too many people are experiencing a decline in vitality due to the demon called complacency. In addition, where that spirit dwells you will find stagnation and disintegration. This could be avoided if we rid ourselves from it before it is too late.

<u>Reference Scriptures</u>

Zephaniah 1:12

At that time, I will search Jerusalem with lamps and punish those who are complacent, who are like wine left on its dregs, who think, 'The LORD will do nothing, either good or bad.'

Ezekiel 30:9

9 "On that day messengers will go out from me in ships to frighten Cush out of her complacency. Anguish will take hold of them on the day of Egypt's doom, for it is sure to come.

Revelation 3:15-21

15 I know your deeds, that you are neither cold nor hot. I wish you were either one or the other! 16 So, because you are lukewarm—neither hot nor cold—I am about to spit you out of my mouth. 17 You say, 'I am rich; I have acquired wealth and do not need a thing.' But you do not realize that you are wretched, pitiful, poor, blind and naked. 18 I counsel you to buy from me gold refined in the fire, so you can become rich; and white clothes to wear, so you can cover your shameful nakedness; and salve to put on your eyes, so you can see. 19 Those whom I love I rebuke and discipline. So be earnest and repent. 20 Here I am! I stand at the door and knock. If anyone hears my voice and opens the door, I will come in and eat with that person, and they with me.

What Happens To The Complacent

Proverbs 1:32

[32] For the waywardness of the simple will kill them, and the complacency of fools will destroy them;

Isaiah 32:9-11

[9] You women who are so complacent, rise up and listen to me; you daughters who feel secure, hear what I have to say! [10] In little more than a year you who feel secure will tremble; the grape harvest will fail and the harvest of fruit will not come. [11] Tremble, you complacent women; shudder, you daughters

who feel secure! Strip off your fine clothes and wrap yourselves
in rags.

Isaiah 64:7
There is no one who calls on Your name, Who arouses
himself to take hold of You; For You have hidden Your face
from us And have delivered us into the power of our iniquities.

1 Corinthians 10:12
Therefore let him who thinks he stands take heed that he
does not fall.

Sermon Twenty

CONSECRATE YOURSELF

Sanctify
Set apart or declare holy

Consecrate
Set apart or dedicate to the service of God

2 Chronicles 5:11-14

[11] The priests then withdrew from the Holy Place. All the priests who were there had consecrated themselves, regardless of their divisions. [12] All the Levites who were musicians—Asaph, Heman, Jeduthun and their sons and relatives—stood on the east side of the altar, dressed in fine linen and playing cymbals, harps and lyres. They were accompanied by 120 priests sounding trumpets. [13] The trumpeters and musicians joined in unison to give praise and thanks to the LORD. Accompanied by trumpets, cymbals and other instruments, the singers raised their voices in praise to the LORD and sang: "He is good; his love endures forever." Then the temple of the LORD was filled with the cloud, [14] and the priests could not perform their service because of the cloud, for the glory of the LORD filled the temple of God.

1 Peter 2:9

[9] But you are a chosen people, a royal priesthood, a holy nation, God's special possession, that you may declare the praises of him who called you out of darkness into his wonderful light.

Exodus 19:14-16

[14] After Moses had gone down the mountain to the people, he consecrated them, and they washed their clothes. [15] Then he said to the people, "Prepare yourselves for the third day. Abstain from sexual relations." [16] On the morning of the third day there was thunder and lightning, with a thick cloud over the mountain, and a very loud trumpet blast. Everyone in the camp trembled.

Job 38:8-12

[8] "Who shut up the sea behind doors when it burst forth from the womb, [9] when I made the clouds its garment and wrapped it in thick darkness, [10] when I fixed limits for it and set its doors and bars in place, [11] when I said, 'This far you may come and no farther; here is where your proud waves halt'? [12] "Have you ever given orders to the morning, or shown the dawn its place,

<u>Consecration Scriptures</u>

Joshua 3:5

[5] Joshua told the people, "Consecrate yourselves, for tomorrow the LORD will do amazing things among you."

Exodus 19:22

[22] Even the priests, who approach the LORD, must consecrate themselves, or the LORD will break out against them."

Exodus 28:41

[41] After you put these clothes on your brother Aaron and his sons, anoint and ordain them. Consecrate them so they may serve me as priests.

Exodus 40:13

[13] Then dress Aaron in the sacred garments, anoint him and consecrate him so he may serve me as priest.

Leviticus 11:44

[44] I am the LORD your God; consecrate yourselves and be holy, because I am holy. Do not make yourselves unclean by any creature that moves along the ground.

Romans 12:1

12 Therefore, I urge you, brothers and sisters, in view of God's mercy, to offer your bodies as a living sacrifice, holy and pleasing to God—this is your true and proper worship.

Romans 6:13

[13] Do not offer any part of yourself to sin as an instrument of wickedness, but rather offer yourselves to God as those who have been brought from death to life; and offer every part of yourself to him as an instrument of righteousness.

1 Samuel 16:5

[5] Samuel replied, "Yes, in peace; I have come to sacrifice to the LORD. Consecrate yourselves and come to the sacrifice with me." Then he consecrated Jesse and his sons and invited them to the sacrifice.

2 Chronicles 29:5

[5] and said: "Listen to me, Levites! Consecrate yourselves now and consecrate the temple of the LORD, the God of your ancestors. Remove all defilement from the sanctuary.

Joel 2:16

[16] Gather the people, consecrate the assembly; bring together the elders, gather the children, those nursing at the breast. Let the bridegroom leave his room and the bride her chamber.

<u>UNITY</u>

Psalm 133:1

[1] How good and pleasant it is when God's people live together in unity!

John 15:9-14

[9] "As the Father has loved me, so have I loved you. Now remain in my love. [10] If you keep my commands, you will remain in my love, just as I have kept my Father's commands and remain in his love. [11] I have told you this so that my joy may be in you and that your joy may be complete. [12] My command is this: Love each other as I have loved you. [13] Greater love has no one than this: to lay down one's life for one's friends. [14] You are my friends if you do what I command.

John 13:35

[35] By this everyone will know that you are my disciples, if you love one another."

COURT DAY FOR THE WICKED

Psalm 94: 1-23

[1] The LORD is a God who avenges. O God who avenges, shine forth. [2] Rise up, Judge of the earth; pay back to the proud what they deserve. [3] How long, LORD, will the wicked, how long will the wicked be jubilant? [4] They pour out arrogant words; all the evildoers are full of boasting.[5] They crush your people, LORD; they oppress your inheritance.

[6] They slay the widow and the foreigner; they murder the fatherless. [7] They say, "The LORD does not see; the God of Jacob takes no notice."[8] Take notice, you senseless ones among the people; you fools, when will you become wise? [9] Does he who fashioned the ear not hear? Does he who formed the eye not see? [10] Does he who disciplines nations not punish? Does he who teaches mankind lack knowledge?

[11] The LORD knows all human plans; he knows that they are futile. [12] Blessed is the one you discipline, LORD, the one you teach from your law; [13] you grant them relief from days of trouble, till a pit is dug for the wicked. [14] For the LORD will not reject his people; he will never forsake his inheritance. [15] Judgment will again be founded on righteousness, and all the upright in heart will follow it.

[16] Who will rise up for me against the wicked? Who will take a stand for me against evildoers? [17] Unless the LORD had given me help, I would soon have dwelt in the silence of death.[18] When I said, "My foot is slipping," your unfailing love, LORD, supported me. [19] When anxiety was great within me, your consolation brought me joy.[20] Can a corrupt throne be allied with you— a throne that brings on misery by its decrees?
[21] The wicked band together against the righteous and condemn

the innocent to death. ²² But the LORD has become my fortress, and my God the rock in whom I take refuge. ²³ He will repay them for their sins and destroy them for their wickedness; the LORD our God will destroy them.

<u>Reference Scriptures</u>

Psalm 10:15-16
¹⁵ Break the arm of the wicked man; call the evildoer to account for his wickedness that would not otherwise be found out. ¹⁶ The LORD is King for ever and ever; the nations will perish from his land.

Deuteronomy 32:43
⁴³ Rejoice, you nations, with his people, for he will avenge the blood of his servants; he will take vengeance on his enemies and make atonement for his land and people.
Isaiah 35:4
⁴ say to those with fearful hearts, "Be strong, do not fear; your God will come, he will come with vengeance; with divine retribution he will come to save you."

Hebrews 10:30
³⁰ For we know him who said, "It is mine to avenge; I will repay," and again, "The Lord will judge his people."

Sermon Twenty-Two

CROSSING YOUR RED SEA

<u>Exodus 14:1-25</u>

Now the LORD spoke to Moses, saying: [2] "Speak to the children of Israel, that they turn and camp before Pi Hahiroth, between Migdol and the sea, opposite Baal Zephon; you shall camp before it by the sea. [3] For Pharaoh will say of the children of Israel, 'They *are* bewildered by the land; the wilderness has closed them in.' [4] Then I will harden Pharaoh's heart, so that he will pursue them; and I will gain honor over Pharaoh and over all his army, that the Egyptians may know that I *am* the LORD." And they did so. [5] Now it was told the king of Egypt that the people had fled, and the heart of Pharaoh and his servants was turned against the people; and they said, "Why have we done this, that we have let Israel go from serving us?" [6] So he made ready his chariot and took his people with him. [7] Also, he took six hundred choice chariots, and all the chariots of Egypt with captains over every one of them.

[8] And the LORD hardened the heart of Pharaoh king of Egypt, and he pursued the children of Israel; and the children of Israel went out with boldness. [9] So the Egyptians pursued them, all the horses *and* chariots of Pharaoh, his horsemen and his army, and overtook them camping by the sea beside Pi Hahiroth, before Baal Zephon. [10] And when Pharaoh drew near, the children of Israel lifted their eyes, and behold, the Egyptians marched after them. So they were very afraid, and the children of Israel cried out to the LORD. [11] Then they said to Moses, "Because *there were* no graves in Egypt, have you taken us away to die in the wilderness? Why have you so dealt with us, to bring us up out of Egypt? [12] *Is* this not the word that we told you in Egypt, saying, 'Let us alone that we may serve the Egyptians'?

For *it would have been* better for us to serve the Egyptians than that we should die in the wilderness."

¹³ And Moses said to the people, "Do not be afraid. Stand still, and see the salvation of the LORD, which He will accomplish for you today. For the Egyptians whom you see today, you shall see again no more forever. ¹⁴ The LORD will fight for you, and you shall hold your peace."

¹⁵ And the LORD said to Moses, "Why do you cry to Me? Tell the children of Israel to go forward. ¹⁶ But lift up your rod, and stretch out your hand over the sea and divide it. And the children of Israel shall go on dry *ground* through the midst of the sea. ¹⁷ And I indeed will harden the hearts of the Egyptians, and they shall follow them. So I will gain honor over Pharaoh and over all his army, his chariots, and his horsemen. ¹⁸ Then the Egyptians shall know that I *am* the LORD, when I have gained honor for Myself over Pharaoh, his chariots, and his horsemen." ¹⁹ And the Angel of God, who went before the camp of Israel, moved and went behind them; and the pillar of cloud went from before them and stood behind them. ²⁰ So it came between the camp of the Egyptians and the camp of Israel. Thus it was a cloud and darkness *to the one,* and it gave light by night *to the other,* so that the one did not come near the other all that night.

²¹ Then Moses stretched out his hand over the sea; and the LORD caused the sea to go *back* by a strong east wind all that night, and made the sea into dry *land,* and the waters were divided. ²² So the children of Israel went into the midst of the sea on the dry *ground,* and the waters *were* a wall to them on their right hand and on their left. ²³ And the Egyptians pursued and went after them into the midst of the sea, all Pharaoh's horses, his chariots, and his horsemen. ²⁴ Now it came to pass, in the morning watch, that the LORD looked down upon the army of the Egyptians through the pillar of fire and cloud, and He troubled the army of the Egyptians. ²⁵ And He took off their

chariot wheels, so that they drove them with difficulty; and the Egyptians said, "Let us flee from the face of Israel, for the LORD fights for them against the Egyptians."

<u>Dry Ground represents</u> God drying up the path before us so we are heading out on firm ground. Jesus is our sure foundation.

<u>The passing through the Red Sea</u> is symbolic of the believer's identification with the death, burial and resurrection of Jesus Christ.

<u>The Rod of Moses represents</u> God's Guidance, power and discipline

<u>REFERENCE SCRIPTURES</u>

Deuteronomy 9:3
[3] Therefore understand today that the LORD your God *is* He who goes over before you *as* a consuming fire. He will destroy them and bring them down before you; so you shall drive them out and destroy them quickly, as the LORD has said to you.

Isaiah 49:25
[25] But this is what the LORD says: "Yes, captives will be taken from warriors,
and plunder retrieved from the fierce; I will contend with those who contend with you, and your children I will save.

Psalm 18:47
[47] He is the God who avenges me, who subdues nations under me,

2 Chronicles 20:15
He said: "Listen, King Jehoshaphat and all who live in Judah and Jerusalem! This is what the LORD says to you: 'Do not be afraid or discouraged because of this vast army. For the battle is not yours, but God's.

DELIVERANCE FROM ZION

<u>Romans 6:17-22</u>

[17] But thanks be to God that, though you used to be slaves to sin, you have come to obey from your heart the pattern of teaching that has now claimed your allegiance. [18] You have been set free from sin and have become slaves to righteousness. [19] I am using an example from everyday life because of your human limitations. Just as you used to offer yourselves as slaves to impurity and to ever-increasing wickedness, so now offer yourselves as slaves to righteousness leading to holiness.

[20] When you were slaves to sin, you were free from the control of righteousness. [21] What benefit did you reap at that time from the things you are now ashamed of? Those things result in death! [22] But now that you have been set free from sin and have become slaves of God, the benefit you reap leads to holiness, and the result is eternal life.

When you are delivered, you become a slave to God. Slavery to God does not imply being forced against our will to do something. It mainly implies that our wills should be bound to do righteousness and live according to God's will in obedience. For example, Paul devoted himself completely to the Lord Jesus Christ and submitted himself entirely to His divine will and in Romans 1:1 he calls himself a bond-servant of Christ Jesus."

In other words Paul did as commanded and whether asked to go somewhere, do something, give, pray, worship or anything else God commands in His words, as delivered (bond servants/slaves) of God, if we love Him, we should obey.

<u>REFERENCE SCRIPTURES</u>

Romans 6:18
You have been set free from sin and have become slaves to righteousness.

Romans 7:4
Therefore, my brothers, you also died to the Law through the body of Christ, that you might belong to another, to Him who was raised from the dead, in order that we might bear fruit to God.

Ephesians 4:12
for the equipping of the saints for the work of service, to the building up of the body of Christ;

1 Peter 2:16
16 Live as free people, but do not use your freedom as a cover-up for evil; live as God's slaves.

Galatians 5:13
For you, brothers, were called to freedom; but do not use your freedom as an opportunity for the flesh. Rather, serve one another in love.

James 1:25
But the one who looks intently into the perfect law of freedom, and continues to do so--not being a forgetful hearer, but an effective doer--he will be blessed in what he does.

Sermon Twenty-Four

DELIVERANCE

Obadiah 1:17
¹⁷ But on Mount Zion will be deliverance; it will be holy, and Jacob will possess his inheritance.

This scripture is all about how you can be delivered from the power of Satan. Many people are in bondage, but don't know how to come out or be delivered. What is deliverance? Deliverance is the eviction of a bad spirit from a place, person or thing. It is to break the chains of wickedness. Deliverance is the destruction of satanic yokes. A yoke is something that ties two animals together and the movement of one depends on the cooperation of the other. If one animal decides to be slow or sluggish, it means that the other one cannot move ahead. Yoke holds back ones progress. Deliverance is the spiritual cleansing of an environment or territory. It means that a school, house, shop, etc., needs deliverance. Clothes we put on need deliverance-cleansing them from spiritual possessions.

WHAT DOES MOUNT ZION REPRESENT?
Mount Zion is described in the Psalms as "the City of our God" and a place that belongs to Him. Situated on a high mountain, it is called "the joy of all the earth" and "the perfection of beauty" (Psalm 48; 50:2). It is the city that God will "establish forever"

Reference scriptures

Psalm 34:4
I sought the LORD, and he answered me; he delivered me from all my fears.

Psalm 40:2

He lifted me out of the slimy pit, out of the mud and mire; he
set my feet on a rock and gave me a firm place to stand.

Psalm 40:13

Be pleased to save me, LORD; come quickly, LORD, to help
me.

Psalm 40:17

But as for me, I am poor and needy; may the Lord think of me.
You are my help and my deliverer; you are my God, do not
delay.

Psalm 107:20

He sent out his word and healed them; he rescued them from
the grave.

Psalm 34:17

The righteous cry out, and the LORD hears them; he delivers
them from all their troubles.

Psalm 107:6

Then they cried out to the LORD in their trouble, and he
delivered them from their distress.

Psalm 50:15

And call on me in the day of trouble; I will deliver you, and you
will honor me

DEMONS ARE REAL

GENESIS 6: 1-4

When human beings began to increase in number on the earth and daughters were born to them. [2] The sons of God saw that the daughters of humans were beautiful, and they married any of them they chose. [3] Then the LORD said, "my spirit will not contend with humans forever, for they are mortal; their days will be a hundred and twenty years." [4] The Nephilim were on the earth in those days—and also afterward—when the sons of god went to the daughters of humans and had children by them. They were the heroes of old, men of renown.

SPIRIT CREATURES—HOW THEY AFFECT US

Getting to know a person usually involves learning something about his family. Similarly, Getting to know Jehovah God includes becoming better acquainted with his angelic family. The Bible calls the angels "sons of God." (Job 38:7) So, what is their place in God's purpose? Have they played a role in human history? Do angels affect your life? If so, how?

WHERE DID ANGELS COME FROM, AND HOW MANY ARE THERE?

Where did angels come from? Colossians 1:16 says: "By means of him [Jesus Christ] all other things were created in the heavens and on the earth." Hence, Jehovah God individually created all the spirit creatures called angels through his firstborn Son. How many angels are there? The Bible indicates that hundreds of millions of angels were created, and all of them are powerful.—Psalm 103:20.

God's Word, the Bible, tells us that when the earth was founded, "all the sons of God began shouting in applause." (Job 38:4-7) Angels thus existed long before humans were created, even before the creation of the earth. This Bible passage also shows that angels have feelings, for it says that they "joyfully cried out together." Note that "all the sons of God" rejoiced together. At that time, all the angels were part of a united family serving Jehovah God.

HOW DOES THE BIBLE SHOW THAT FAITHFUL ANGELS ARE INTERESTED IN HUMAN ACTIVITIES?

Ever since they witnessed the creation of the first humans, faithful spirit creatures have shown keen interest in the growing human family and in the outworking of God's purpose. (Proverbs 8:30, 31; 1 Peter 1:11, 12) With the passing of time, however, the angels observed that most of the human family turned away from serving their loving Creator. No doubt, this saddened the faithful angels. On the other hand, whenever even one human returns to Jehovah, "joy arises among the angels." (Luke 15:10) Since angels have such deep concern for the welfare of those who serve God, it is no wonder that Jehovah has repeatedly used angels to strengthen and protect his faithful servants on earth. (Read Hebrews 1:7, 14.) Consider some examples.

An angel protecting Daniel in the lions' pit
"My God sent his angel and shut the mouth of the lions."—Daniel 6:22
Two angels helped the righteous man Lot and his daughters to survive the destruction of the wicked cities of Sodom and Gomorrah by leading them out of that area. (Genesis 19:15, 16)

HOW DO ANGELS PROTECT GOD'S PEOPLE TODAY?

Today, angels no longer appear visibly to God's people on earth. Although invisible to human eyes, God's powerful angels still protect his people, especially from anything spiritually harmful. The Bible says: "The angel of Jehovah camps all around those fearing Him, and he rescues them." (Psalm 34:7) Why should those words be of great comfort to us? Because there are dangerous, wicked spirit creatures who want to destroy us!

SPIRIT CREATURES WHO ARE OUR ENEMIES

One of the angels developed a desire to rule over others and thus turned against God. Later this angel became known as Satan the Devil. (Revelation 12:9) During the 16 centuries after he deceived Eve, Satan succeeded in turning away from God nearly all humans except a few faithful ones, such as Abel, Enoch, and Noah.—Hebrews 11:4, 5, 7.

HOW DID SOME ANGELS BECOME DEMONS?

In Noah's day, other angels rebelled against Jehovah. They left their place in God's heavenly family, came down to the earth, and took on fleshly bodies. Why? We read at Genesis 6:2: "The sons of the true God began to notice that the daughters of men were beautiful. So they began taking as wives all whom they chose." But Jehovah God did not allow the actions of these angels and the resulting corruption of mankind to go on. He brought upon the earth a global flood that swept away all wicked humans and preserved only his faithful servants. (Genesis 7:17, 23) Thus, the rebellious angels, or demons, were forced to abandon their fleshly bodies and return to heaven as spirit creatures. They had put themselves on the side of the Devil, who thus became "the ruler of the demons."—Matthew 9:34.

HOW DEMONS MISLEAD

To mislead people, the demons use tactics and strategies. This is how they involve us with them in a direct way. These tactics do for the demons what bait does for fishermen. A fisherman uses a variety of baits to catch various kinds of fish. Similarly, wicked spirits use different forms of strategies to bring all sorts of people under their influence.

<u>HOW TO RESIST WICKED SPIRITS</u>

Paul said, "Take up the large shield of faith, with which you will be able to extinguish all the wicked one's [Satan's] burning arrows." (Ephesians 6:16) The stronger our shield of faith, the greater our resistance to wicked spirit forces will be.—Matthew 17:20.

Wicked spirits are dangerous, but we need not live in fear of them if we oppose the Devil and draw close to God by doing His will. (Read James 4:7, 8.) The power of wicked spirits is limited. They were punished in Noah's day, and they face their final judgment in the future. (Jude 6) Remember, too, that we have the protection of Jehovah's powerful angels. (2 Kings 6:15-17) Those angels are deeply interested in seeing us succeed in resisting wicked spirits. Let us therefore stay close to Jehovah and his family of faithful spirit creatures. (1 Peter 5:6, 7; 2 Peter 2:9) Then we can be sure of victory in our fight against wicked spirit creatures.

<u>Appreciation</u>

I would like to extend a very heartfelt thank you, first to God the Father, Son and Holy Spirit who directed me in writing this book. To my immediate family for their constant support. To Apostle Anthony Greaves, Evangelist Cora Beckles, Miss. Valarie Deane, and Prophetess Debbie Isaac who saw the anointing upon my life when no one else saw it.

I am very grateful to Pastor Cheryl Harewood for believing in my calling and I would like to extend my sincerest gratitude to Anthony Devonish, Reverend Michelle Marshall, Reverend Wasim Worrell, Reverend Kerrie Worrell, Reverend Waldron, Minister Waldron, Evangelist Arlene, Minister Maria Clarke and the members of the congregation for standing with me in ministry.

About The Author

Apostle Marguerite Breedy-Haynes was born in St. Lucia to one Barbadian parent and one St. Lucian parent and is the seventh of sixteen children. She lived in Barbados since childhood and is married with three children.

Saved by Jesus who visited her in a vision, she was taken to hell, and there she was given a mandate by God not to let anyone go to that place. She then gave her life completely over to Him and was anointed as an End Time Prophet. Her ministry began by giving tracts on the streets of Barbados for over 3 years until God promoted her.

Saving The Lost At Any Cost, End Time Ministries' was started at her house and has now become an international ministry with branches based in Barbados, South Carolina, St. Lucia and several others which are being birthed around the world. Hundreds came to her from all over Barbados. Their lives were changed through the deliverance of the Word of God, many were healed and demons were cast out.

As an End Time Prophet, she was called to preach the gospel of the second coming of the Lord Jesus Christ. She has travelled the world ministering in various churches and crusades, teaching and admonishing others to live holy lives before God. She is known for not compromising the Word of God and believes in living what she preaches. Her desire is to win souls for the end times and to snatch God's children from the hands of the enemy.

I pray that this book has been a blessing to you. For more information on the author, her ministry and her books, please contact us or visit us at:

Telephone: (246) 249-3265

Website: www.maggie365.wixsite.com/savingthelost

Address: Saving The Lost At Any Cost End Time Ministries
Barbados, West Indies

Facebook:
https://www.facebook.com/savingthelostinternational/

Twitter: https://twitter.com/savingthelost1

Medium: https://medium.com/@savingthelost

Email: savingthelost@live.com

Instagram: Savingthelostatanycost